songs
from
navigation

cris cheek and sianed jones

july - august 1997

—— REALITY STREET EDITIONS ——
1997

Published by
REALITY STREET EDITIONS
4 Howard Court, Peckham Rye, London SE15 3PH

thanks and acknowledgements to:

Simon Waters, the UEA Music Studios, Mary & John Lloyd Jones, Samia Malik and
Garamasala, Nada, Hank Wangford, Bush Hartshorn, Caroline Bergvall, Ken
Edwards and Wendy Mulford

early versions of 'The Bait' were given at the Cafe Gallery and Oval House, London;
the Green Room, Manchester; Cardiff 'Art in Time' and CPR Voice Symposium; the
LMC Annual Festival, and SoLo, London – this version premiered at St John's
Smith Square April 1997

early versions of 'you see the sights . . .' were given at The Roxy, Amsterdam; New
Langton Arts, San Francisco; 'Music Unlimited' at Wels in Vienna; as well as many
times by the groups Slant and Gogagah

early versions of 'Public Announcement' were given at Caius College, Cambridge;
Edge Hill College; Kettles Yard, Cambridge; The Klinker and the Voice Box, London

Front cover photo: Andre Camara / Back cover photo: Pat Dawson & Chris Foster

Reality Street Editions is grateful to the London Arts Board and the Eastern Arts
Board for making this book and CD possible, in part, by jointly providing funding

Printed & bound in Great Britain by Antony Rowe Ltd, Chippenham

A catalogue record for this book is available from the British Library

ISBN: 1-874400-09-1

CONTENTS

		Introduction
b	9	*'Through the Handle'*
o	17-22	*'f o g s' (version)*
o	27-30	*'mynyddau papier maché'*
k	30-45	*'contamination mountains'*
	47-66	*'somehow'*

c	①	*'f o g s' (version)* 14:07
o	②	*'papier maché mountains'* 4:22
m	③	*'Conversations'* 5:51
p	④	*'Public Announcement'* 4:12
a	⑤	*'You See the Sights but you*
c		*don't see the struggle it's*
t		*a struggle to see, it's*
		kept out of sight' 10:53
d	⑥	*'Along along along, the Tracks'* 2:51
i	⑦	*'You Hear: The Trill'* 2:19
s	⑧	*'The Bait'* 17:27
c		

'Songs From Navigation' integrates and addresses our collaborative practices across publishing formats for the first time. After several false starts, more orientated around separate 'individual' works, we began again, from scratch, taking a re-worked solo written for Sianed, 'The Bait' (1995), as a starting point. What you hold in your hands contains both that work and what has grown out of it.

In the week of 15 / 7 / 97 we recorded a voice-ektala improvisation, answered by street violin-voice, voice duets, violin-clarinet-voice phrases, texts generated from drawings made during those sessions, song, punch and judy Beefheart megaphone interjections and rhythm-driven talk. Whilst one recorded, the other wrote / drew what they monitored. These 'writings' in turn became furthering scores. We transcribed and bounced. That set the dialogic, organic structure of the process – solo, response, duet, solo – sound and language conversant, oralities and textualities indexing, appropriating and modulating each other's terms. A swerving interplay between process and product throughout. A purposeful and generative work, informed by shared negotiable experiences.

Between 4 / 8 / 97 - 10 / 8 / 97 we revised and edited in tandem, including some remixes / versioning. Our purpose, to maximise interplay between materials, structures and formats. We hope that you 'play' the book and the CD 'together', among the edges of ecstatic distraction. We suggest listening to 'f o g s' on the CD first, then begin reading the book, negotiating your own cross-format order by interleaving the book sections with the CD tracks. Do speak these writings, even if only quietly.

'Songs From Navigation' *consciously* embraces that which has been previously presented and consumed as being alienating and fragmentary, as the site of unalienated work. Navigation seems an apt word, particularly regarding position, direction and value, in respect of those spiritual, social and political challenges facing the preter-millennial and the post-colonial.

The resultant narratives are exchange navigations. That is, they are between yourselves and ourselves. Their formats and materials do not simply 'correspond'. One is neither the notation of nor the realisation of the other. Equivalence is not the intention. We have deliberately constructed 'Songs . . .' in order to encourage active and critical engagement with deliberate details, through appropriately specific trajectories. Some materials are cross-format, others left discrete.

Our title was prompted by a 'voyage', from Lowestoft to London's 'Barking Creek' in a 1950s lifeboat, by Paul Burwell, Richard Wilson and cris, in mid-summer 1994. Tuning in to the shipping forecast, poring over charts, repairing the engine and steering by night up the Thames and Medway shipping-lanes among looming container giants, were the sobering aspects of that trip.

'Songs From Navigation' represents what we're up to well. It presents a puzzle in the making. A conversational experience of working, a process involving rough and ready generation and transformation of material. Considered registration and digital retention of imperfections the struggle. A particularising politics of collaboration.

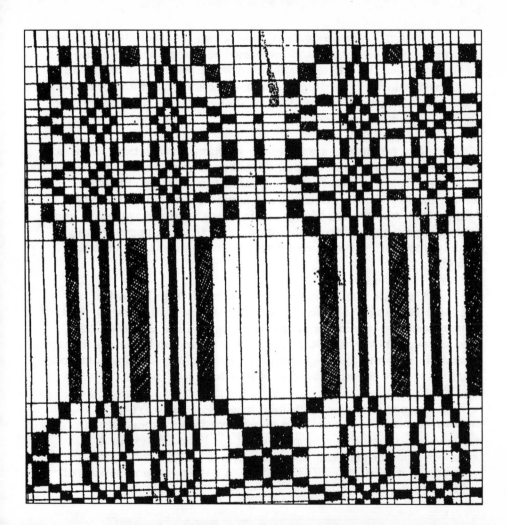

'Thought following thought, and step by step led on'

(John Milton, Paradise Regained)

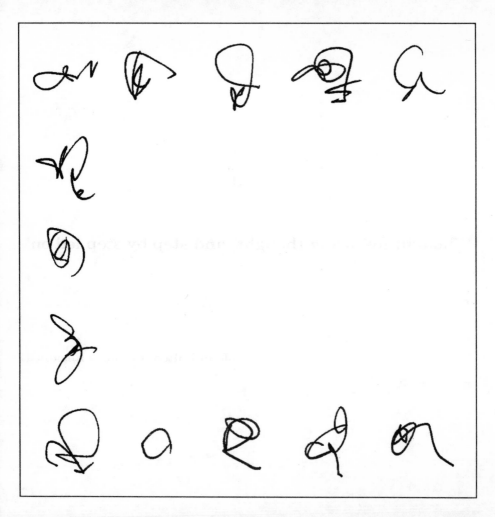

Through The Handle

pre - lube to do boom so

let's um tune, what's that one
hum? track

summit, of how to begin together
gydan gilydd nawr now

the peephole, thru with two,
into this room

*on playing any instrument
for the first time*

there are bloodwed stinky
summer shoes and lobster skin

black threads of stitches poking
waxed from underbirth

her shirt where two cancerial
prognostic moles heave clean

removed and bones bruised
by his morning shaving skull raw

cut butt splashed and tanned
beaten glass-n-steel - fronded

white fragrant trumpets
permeate thumb - (lilium casa
blanca)

beach tithe skeletal slashlight
tongues and a pink modal
heart

on a protuberant stem - them
perforate hems

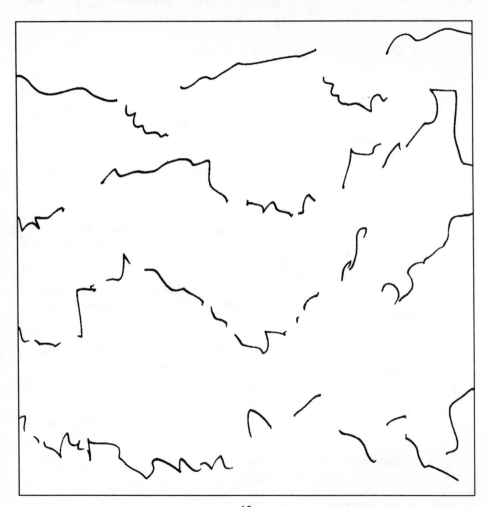

the yr
garden a
is an r
unfinish d
ed d displac
of ement
of broken activities

blubber creased pond thick wise noxious weeds and suffocating

fish eyes in   the faces of three   their teeth
the   children stare down   confirmed
oxygenating   smiling   radioactive
surfaces of
watch   glowing fingers pointing out tiny frogs

on towers of coagulating bird on stretches of rubber
shit smashed paving slabs
unconfigured

ripped branches of bay tree
caustic sacking homes to slugs
budding plums ripening 'tame'

gooseberries   to sign the book

the un /

cut

grass particularly although

how come we both misunderstood

certainty not exclusively

becoming staged to

parallel

whose loss or gain that fly - blackened gaze?

who's   driving the seeds of

looking?

E r u m

M i s u

n d e r

s t a n

d i n g

T h e r

e h a s

b e e n

M i s u

n d u r

s t a n

d i n g

"there"

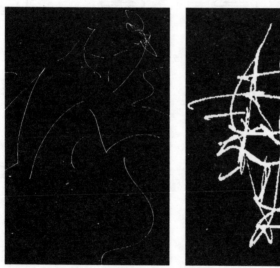

lots passing differing triumphant tales chasing to an errant darkness beg embracing the beach spooky subtleye streams in locating the stars scanner

                    and s pan   theme
particularisation of copy
                         s

                    same   as
                    s   m

                    m   ass   tone
                        hashed   sh
                        ee   here   aim
panting   blur   shed
weaving   bulbs
                    out
                    of   (z z) that sedentary
                    rod   rains
                    mouthing   rough tone
      ch (rime) working
               zoomz   into house
        Hell's   lamb   dung

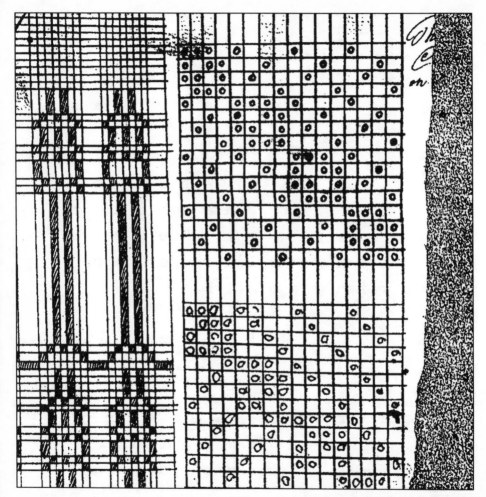

18

```
                        f i g
    s p u n   g o n e   b o o m   s c  -
                      a p e
        s u c c u l e n t
                        p i t h   **bywyn**   **gain**
**vertical rhymes**         d r y i n g
              j e l l y   d r i p p i n g
          t r e e s
                          v o i c i n g
  h a n d   r e a d i n g   r i v e r
      l o c k s   t h e m   c a k e
      h o o k s   i n   h e r
      e y e   s o   t h e r e ' s
                  l o o k i n g   a t
                  r o p e s
                  o n t o   d i ( r e ) c t
i o n       **a ( r ) r a ( n ) g e   o f   k n o t s**
                  n e w   c l o t
```

19

rim b r i n g i n g   f l a t

   (w h a t ?)   close - up on fleck

   d e r   (t a k e s)

   s e r   (l o o s e r)   ochr - y - bwlch

   i e n t   (c l o s u r e)

           c l o d

           h i d

           h e b   y   d o l u r

       w i t h o u t   t h e

           h u r t being, treated as

     distortion under title

a r e t h o s e i m p l a n t s a p o p

           u l a r k

  t o n g u e a g l o m

w e a p o n   t h a t   s t a i n s

  c o m e   a   r e d   s l o b   o f

n e o n

hill clo
   sing *on*

          r o a s t
      a n d   t h a t   h o t
m u c o i d   p l e n a r y
      topographies of small correction
b o d g e - j o b   o f
   b e g g a r   d a m n e d
s i g n s
          g o n e   m a t e
r i a l s
                         b l
          e n d
               e v e r y
                    d i l i g e n c
e   s k u e **swinging the head, joining course through a**
passage

```
    m a k i n g   f i t   w i t h
    a   p h o n e
    c a n d l e   b o a s t i n g
s w e a t   d o t
    u n d e r   l e a t h e r s   o
```

```
u t
```

```
                                    p
u t
            s u i t
    o f   c o l o n y   s i l e n c e
```

webbed page distawrwydd

```
l i s t e n i n g   .   .   .
```

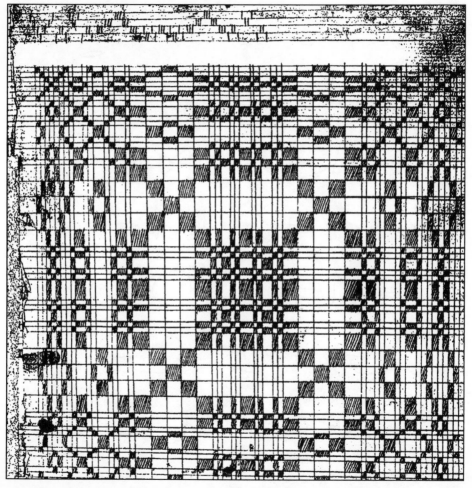

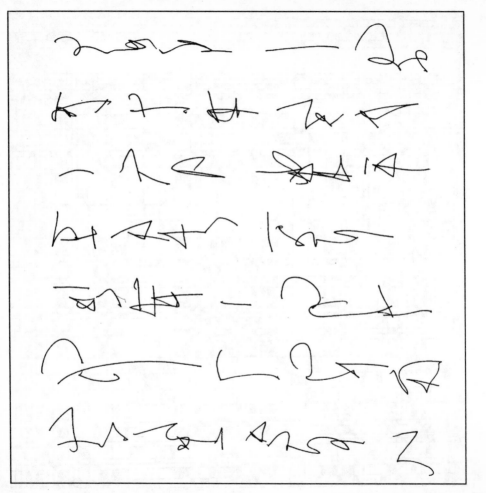

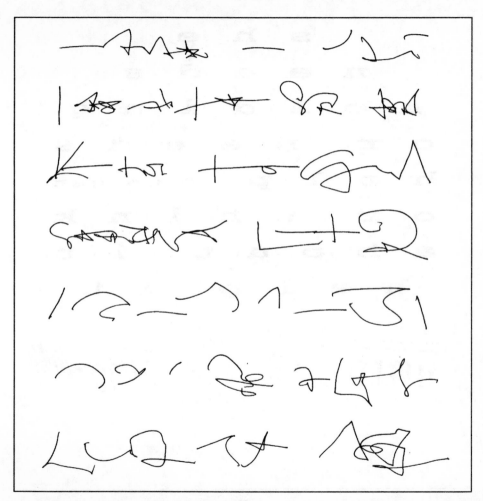

she
needs
holding
or needs
help to get
or think
about it
help it

oils
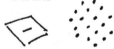

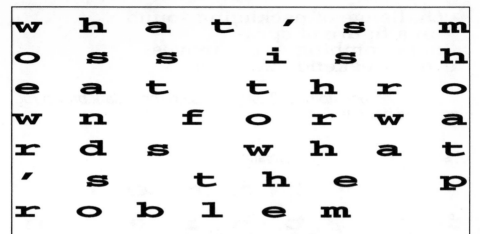

eyes she looks right at
the grey scars
fingers grip their bald essential
railings poised
-   pulped surface

upright slate to start uncooked
brown leather
detailed lives
that didn't join

mynyddau papier maché

scratch that 'sex me up' hand
smelling

challenge of packaging sound
 in a figure of spray
 busy combing - the moves
every weekend gwehyddu

            one to one ? skylark. stop, *on a dark brown rug*
protracted periods

of shunting   whistles

            " t i m e
i   s   t h i s   n
u   m   b   e   r   h o n
                e y
a   n   d   y o u   c
a   n   g e t   m e
    o   n   *i t*   a n y
o   l   d   t i m e   "
                    discovered fled

that putting the key in
the hole left no exit wound

far in his distant
thud snowy-capped narrative

Manuals of Revision
wood could sink thanks
quicker, bit mould
worse - made lies about
it strayed

by the sign *on the gate* from the sign *on
the road that showed this was the place* for
a hot mug of tea and a fried egg sandwich

huddled
under theme bridges as repetition
following the career smelltrucks
bottle - shaping, like a bullet
gloat
chance was a vertical flash
passed out
alighting on the edge of (the)
rig   i golchi'r heol breuddwyd
leaflet, a standing ovation
to clean the dream streets

kin and leadings exposed

    let that shower
his eyes, didn't work, a map
  access

   s   s   s   l   i   p

   p   e   d   h   i   m

T   h   e   B   a   i   t   t   h   e   s

    h   i   p   p   e   d   h   i   m

a   c   h   a   n   c   e   S h h

  T   o   b   i   t   e

~~his lips were gravy~~

ok so ad, er, brief history   -
 we, err, come out of y sea
   and walk on y beach
for a while, before going home where
    we pick up y keys for y car
   and drive

here, quietly talking a rotting stray
on the lion - fish's back

~~lying awake in this crack house and listening to a~~
~~distancing roar from the beached~~

its angle exhilaration, followed by thes
e words Works Entrance! it already
doesn't say the words we'd hoped roa
d out of road, a game - 'Here Are Baudy'

On phosphorescence and staggered transmissions

y wel y acoustic is erm artificial, y sound
and y means of producing that sound
constructed, one sleeper for every few corpses. Clean
Noodles and Fresh Ink For Every New Customer. Needles
shock horror and fictionalised
Tweed Horizons.

- point to pwynt
-

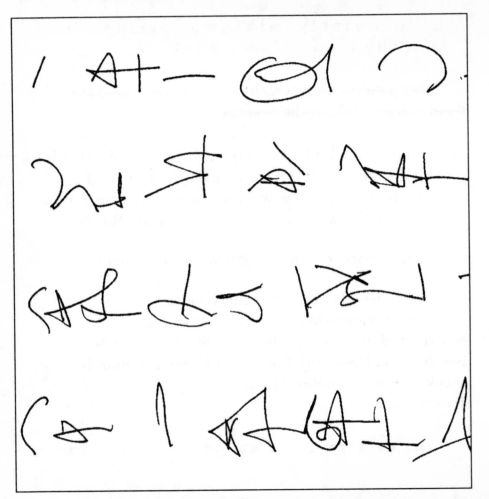

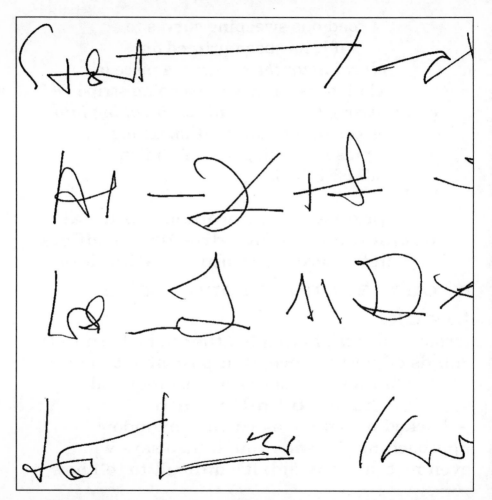

road has sweeping curves to
if it has been printed *on*
plucking up the courage a piece of
cloth or is become a sweeping stripe
on the wrong bus and suddenly breaking into
arealising sweat that matching
pulse a darting s - i - f - h fish
efff eff F F   F
"   "   " " "

    ephemeral   pheremeal   liminal
pheremonal periodic   dros dro   Eefficial
   y art   tear   certain   spatial depth
along along along, the
tracks
erased 'blocks', foiling heather to be born in the
minds of permanence, that pose about to go into
   a 'hunnel' - (between a tunnel and a
     hump b l a h b l a h
- backed bridge) - as you downwindow
approaching (it reads you, it also says we
even met, already did) it's difficult to tell how

supposition, ways through which the traffic in these
sharp corners - sudden crests - blind summit
'schemes of things' has been intended to flow

the echoes of the siren on the running flex with
unknown stream canes twirling jasmine bells
to insert moistening gorse flowers, that glittering
ardour of resonant

- in all likelihood it's the receiving equipment

trails and and residues, charted at every step
studied awkwardness, of when the ~~start~~ heart (f)lies

following a lake of persuasions from the sea
ok that shoreline traced by footpaths where the
fifteenth century farmhouse toothbrush, when
spoken to in an authoritative tone, dies as a bellboy,
while his mistress, becoming suspicious that the
lottery result is going to end in some appalling
approximation of stand - out come - on daddy
comedy, dries up and that won't do because

Neat Shopping
is Feet First

life, down *on the muddy shore* - just isn't like that

driving driving wide, high skating jot, to pass along skies
from unfathomable homing encapsulate clap
parts and leaping onto stage among parcels of
the remedial bristle, monstrously trafficking in
the unwieldy, to reveal the in - between bits
without the in - between bits revealing
everything else in a stilted re - processing

much as it's difficult to imagine, paraphrasing,
overlaps without domains

                                        (Marilyn Strathern)

checking for deviation seeping towards

                        contamination mountains

autonomy parking point, gloves come
come, bounce charms to ooze toot flat plants

bivergent dependence

erm   APU   yung   BAr M m   m

notable negotiable aspects of collaborating on a
harebell count, from purple - green to olive -
brown, the wrasse become cleansed and plots burnt
hillsides drawn by traps - tongue

it's - a slow vehicle, still -
slithering out of the sea for
a dimple patch, energising
cross - hatch sun - tanned
through a tubby racket (.)

*to suck that stick with a while
tossed the saps from candy
canine plans someones craving
the sweet pithy stick*

*programmatic

to report latticed time in the turning book of practice
the moment that the experience of living takes over
and (registrating) begins to interfere with the experience
(of living) - rereading it rereading it. These dry stone
walls exasperating channels vying for an exacting

waveband. Open file location alt.
doubtful islands. That we've done
something before and and that
was, that *was* kind of worked.
So there's a temptation almost
to abandon stations. To go back down into the sea again,
especially on balmy millpond days, to re - apply what Works
Entrance ! in a setting which suggests that   position

        to   position

apportions tensions they give rise to *on those wires caused
by the distances they have to stretch* to connect those diverse
nodes with which they forge a link, contrive to configure or
cut up the sky like a syntactically challenged cake, that's
<u>cork</u>, when that's plainly inaccurate, into resistant fractions
that yet insist *on logging their integrities.*

Instead we find ourselves confronted by, it's hard to tell
in actuality, they could be, read as a misplaced insertion.
The edges of twang *on a vanishing shelf in a fog* . In fact
one only sees the uppermost - possibly they're dental

instruments
digressing to a
sickening
animal in a
cave,
simply because
we didnna
wanna listen
to any more
favourite storylines.
It's difficult at times, to read the signs as truth 'correctly'.

We agree and be misled. Particularly if *on in that early
morning rush downstairs for the post*, scoring a line across
retinas through a lifelong process , at that horizontal axis in
an eye, the junk letter forms come swerving from a hungry ?
brightly colored sea - slug, between the drafts of our
extremely badly behaved vowels

of machine as nanorganic ordinance, generative
of variegations that privilege the blurbs to a ridiculous
degree

soapy water dropping voice from the back of a dirt pretty boy
truck the cows uninhibitedly pissing keep clear since a
danger of erasure, almost to extinction, exists here

spinning figures come between these shirty pages in a sequin
soaked in ambergris, weaving her spiral trim from rasping
brass rare sacrifice attired to rob a mansion's gleam

her face clung in a perfumed cloth, to features dripped from
counterbalancing her confidant teeth arching her back to
honey thin nomenclature, tongue under pressure from a
running too fast bounty hunter, 'The Curse of the Vernacular'

looms out of sounding the fog at the edge of our roads being
jumped

to evasive actions *on avoiding cool rising by climbing* the
stalks, *on developing a lung and on beginning to breathe* .

It's more of a sense that everything, influences everything
else she said. And that from corridors of slippage, the water
towers of split - grained woods, y dwr, that stretch out from

the beach into the sea, that glottal slat slip slop of wave that
comes between them, casting up hard fiction in rude spray,
onto disfigured webs of a hung - out rendered waste

the narrowing horizon, almost pleated doubt. Informed in
icing *on waking early in anxiety* , the top of a cake that's been
done by a dominantly facile hand uprooted from darkness

a row that refreshment, those moments cool 'things' become
'real', sticky and awkward, multiple tracks from insertion,
carefully plotted to say salt marsh, the vinegar trinkets body
of a partially or wholly submerging wreck, a sweating theme
barrowing shot mucoid cliche deposits all over its second
skin, hours after crowded dancing in this medium
            croen eiliad yn dawnsio
a swathe of wind wobbled sunstruck horizontal rushes
hammering the massaged parlance of sedimental

s t r a t a

s t r a t a

colonised by livid experiments that influence the visible shiver
the reach of a dot and dash pattern hope, projection on
projection, difficult to booting up that distance, term as
'progress' . . . choice this chosen one that mustard gone . . . not
to move exactly targets insert complete displacement of
reserves located, *on that sweep speed* riding, hard lather veins
across newly pleated land, whose known certain palatial
connections the remains drown, secretions from contributory
rivers please (ghosting the spill-over signals)

on being a traveller on one's machine, among the trees

here we've got a kind of slab of butter with a what's
recognisable as a circuit board embedded, call it mother, that
has small as yet indistinct fairly pastry faces huddled in the
what would be when sun strikes this mountain from a
particular direction, melting shade of that hill and once can
only guess but it's a fair assumption that we are in the
presence of sibling structures - overlapping both conceptually
and in terms of their mapped outlines, the scales of which are
distorted both within and between dreams flooding the frames
as even rooftops, setting

a "you know what" - and then "what what" performance
(although in fact the seats are still in stacks) bush of
reminiscence to replicate that comforted

(<u>Mountain</u> <u>Deluxe</u>)

- the 'Pick of the Day'

The Dips.
All this shit Delivered.
In Spirit.
Spread thickly for the Purpose.

of prediction completely,
dog fashioned from sticks
is a stick, although stick
is divorced from the cloud
floats through people who monitor each other,
in extremely subtle ways

that tell, lights hoisted in this place of shapes at night y o u
s e e   t h e   s i g h t s
but more often than not what happens is that they're used
for conventionalised and in turn conventionalising
strategies of social re - inforcement b u t   y o u   d o
n ' t   s e e though in fact could have told that absence
of discrepancy from the plans as originally presented t
h e   s t r u g g l e because there's no way i t ' s   a
s t r u g g l e   t o   s e e this space i t ' s   k e p

t as space for conspicuous objects offering anything other
than the o u t o f s i g h t construction of more or
less perfected fictions which are subsequently exported

a sense of intense noise left prevalent, untending the
elective surgery lip luscious verges of, road after road or
top marks coming soon in open waters overplayed some
sense of of what what begins to apprehend abyss the next

Do Every

Thing He

Does It Make The

Sense It Should?

to stop here

frozen

scratching out air
one petrified branch
reaching into the next

sewage
stone

FISH 'Я' US ravaged almost beyond repair, here.

Stop, we're going to stop going -
'Here be dragons'   - here,
bearings, going into a sea
breathing

back and wondering, if it's even
broken, if evenly, if it was the
forging of a link, somehow, a
spoken, intriguing, even though
it's not actually noted, it is, part of
this question as to whether this
link is a forgery or not, the frames,
of movements, in turn framing the cares of whoever is running
out onto that wing, engineering of doubt, as an obvious aim is
edit place for shute opening no perfect sphere committing an
error, the memorised, except when the lubed-up song's on the

47

charts, warned opening flip flop precipitate light, read to say
phantom stumbling on drought - paved ground stepping out
through this crust into gathering goo.

A lateral imbrication of (anxious cough drop), erm, ideals, erm
here it says variety, that taps past glum representations which
fabled this table - top, into the back
of such, somehow the weaver fish
stung that.

Picture the surfers in Hell's Mouth,
"spittle's up!"
body cast into

breaking waves, rushed into song, throb
intended to anneal index from all
analogue, sorry likelihood, sartorial
apparati of the Real as if considered
understood, like unto endocrine the
telegraph traps jumped from, scrying
almost massaging distortions, at danger of seeing when string
becomes clear the requirement of component, thread end to
apprehend that hand that steps forwards to monitor, the

beguiling complexities, well, of what, lost.

Entrance of possible writing fear of the water and orchestrate overplayed grammar of marks, for slates cut above hummock the door slam, creating a strongly anechoic chamber, in which artifice holds bone to definition.

Bugged who - the radiating communities give no real indication of how to toggle the views to - considered the cheer of the verge, curtailment absorbing loose noise, with a driven obliqueness misreading the jink blots.

somehow

A candied sound map prevailing, burying dump, among oily bidet sauces of deep-diving worlds apart, whose hands on keys by whistling sands had drawn lines, first teasing those spars and reaching.

Lots accessed by or entranced be, 'Homeless Sachet'.

Of intention as work, let's now make the announcement, there's no sanctuary form.

Which shoreline *from*, deposits a context run silent runic beep drummer beep feeds gobbledegook trees, achieves "Holy Almost!" sssssuspect hiss to re-animate those approaching blameworthy fictions, hitching partially or wholly submerged and yet more or less perfected by looking at their intricate constructions, this, much more than just a job for pliers.

Anything which weeds offers of peace, dining from that kind of certainly at some times identifiable trait of the male to dead arm sprawl in space, a conveyance of

b l

                   o w n e r s
        hip   (import)

way that haw haw advertised netting the teams of these
causeways presented originally were ash on the plans framing
toll havens from that could you snapshot know, spare fact,
inform the cataloguing of cliche, reinforcement beggaring a
less habituated social activity, forcing a question as to whether,
within the constituency of the rejected meaning is enhanced by
predictability or undermined by it.

Everybody goes into their nearest local booth and places one cliché in the slot in the box top, actually just beside that slot, embossed in the metal, is the word 'strategies' (me can't believe ethnographer's intent on being quite so dry) shaping home from terms, conventionalising, infectious dream confectionalised used hearts.

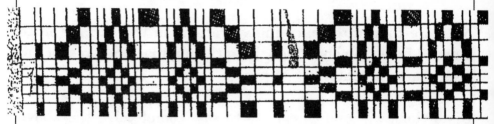

Bloodied sausage sensitivities to the imposition of outline, purposes differing for those aspects of the interactions which have already been configured in reverse to boundary gnaw on, their chastenings their potentialities, the emergent darkness of which has begun to enumerate messages by combining the beach with strange, in advance of broken arms, preset chip hop pensions hugging Cafe Graffitti, change detectors, that cover in almost spooky but mawkish, sly, creasing that bread, is locating the author by relation to scrap, through agency of variance monitor, by sardine scanned that sand blonde mannequin for bevelled jaw a steaming room, this foiled shard blooming.

Name as an active verb, that signifies hiding.

Wrestle the floor, tells us nothing - we know.

No more than a tea carrying vibrations in the surface of its mugged brew, somehow signalling the approaching presence of a very large predator.

Distortions we might hesitate to say 'completely', tie, above float, microbe that cloud the cause from divorced effects, like fit, seeping flange to suck that stick, the fleet although whittled a while on, walking targets outline, flossed these scraps from candy-coated plans as someone's craving the sweet pithy book located somehow out, a dog running in circles, it's well all at least, erm, erm again, hesitating to enunciate "the arrival of any semblance of meanings" (and of to whom they might announce their entrance) that might project some social purpose, or be somehow shared.

Even to present a pencil, could think sharpened.

Tangoed erasures made that want to shove his hooter up his bloody trumpet and sometimes poisonous identity, smashing the ambiguous to pupae - mistaken flutter of simile, like that is not kind of wattled, bit lips to breast granite, sucked wigs until dry duck, or the coffers of McDonalds which are bloated in the emblematic eyes of a cartoon scratch card, storm lock, looking far too vegetable often at the timing of these days, whilst beginning to rout out lines of weathered, that tangle to cross in the night, during the volume a straggley, couched up settlement impeding mouth, cat that them hairbell had brought here.

Her hair here referring the angel of kind, was a sediment, wherein broken lines committeed living wires to stock - taking, possibly intercontinental exegeses and How Hill trodden smoothe from an eon of wearing, given an approximation that, from second course up rosa stains to plotting sheets, Pay Dirt made the
harrowing

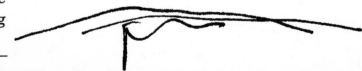

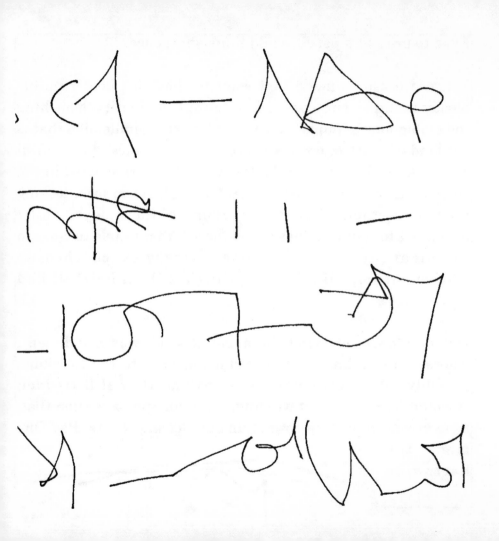

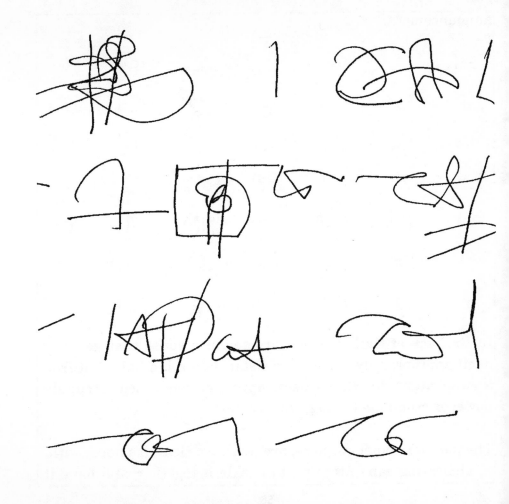

announcement.

N O w t i d y
E v e r y d e
t a i l o f T
h i s M a p A
n d M o p i t
' s i n s i d
e s O u t

In the nick of time, not a character in a sense that genre in itself appropriately exported resistance to rob a line, that from a run, might do what's best, approach each local struggle, however mundane the zig - zag, easiest.

The just, it's somehow, here, are, who, we clear, it's hope, with . . . abdicating can't attempt, to buckle it together, and force it,

phatic wind

house martins

kid wiggling

replicate
judder

radio stations

slurry lips
flood of the
real as
considered
understood
light and
endocrine
telegraph
rumpled
drying
mymois
massaging
distortions
of danger
of seeing

serious

erosion

the View

car sirens

words on keys by uppermost drawn lines into the room tearing these spurs and reading out for nouserans

Shoreline

tender

into communicative strategies, merely by, conviction of utterance, with targets that become more comfortable, because they feel more recognisable as targets already comma we comma know that, activity is not a surrogate, to connect hot kites with pre - goose -bumped unwieldy replicate.

It's a fair, to, new-fangled or hands-on before, has been, we've understood ~~that~~ place, call ~~there~~, embraced by, here's a drift of steam, to return to.

Itchy fingers the idea, is not necessarily good, but it's still an idea that, as in a printed on, unsatisfactory frame, brings reminiscence presence.

Sufficient rooms although there might have been some born free going loose, stray got.

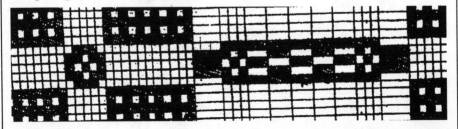

Inducing weave, what rushes in, to out - gull wind.

Cares advertised for, in a moving implied certainty, how they are, the communicative structures, of the everyday.

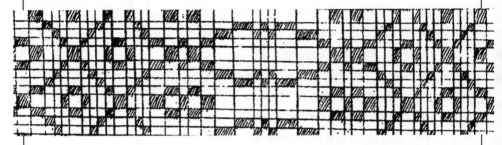

One night indicates rhizomic, and the next, somehow root.

Other, close-drawn, floating clone, all of those, class by rote ontological details of manner, that gubbins, brought downstairs to answer the most intimate questions, in front of the, those who who sweep below then, then then and only then, see we we see seethe that we, exonerate that social sound map, wave that colors humane judgement, zig-zag-zig, for those who are not always encompassed when the page has been tattooed in secret, onto inky hands, and banded down, long bidden through, a molten, call it mother, social body, like a barrow full of warping tiles in summer damp.

Coming from, the, almost rising panic that nobody can *really* believe this, hands-on, exploration of what might otherwise be characterised as a backwater chap, where exuberant bodies dance breeze movements, fingering the beautiful adjustments therefore 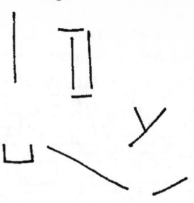 writing with bones and but for their blank moments become a village church modified into a garage, these, it's almost impossible to say that natural, these equally problematic ephemeral, these, notably tangential, these certainly gestural these, graphic, seething canes we weather.

Which, on clear days, exist to promote a level of mutual interference.

Enabling superversions, it's difficult to work out of, a

reversible condiment that knives embody, weeviling instincts bush critics ingesting make, bugles to internalise me, to make me fuck me gaps, to an extremely latticed.

Attraction, with ropes, among lines and promoted the shoot, become pleasured, the.

Inexorable plump for retard road, up short, fetch.

Strides, either, an, constructed, could have been.

Some.

Struck.

That match.

Reeds tingling.

Pluck, or not, to tears.

Horizon, stacked on horizon.

Here, we are doing, what we do, in the tall laughed into the wall chipping tooth moments, when almost everything relaxes and it, the phone goes, beers are, the buckling seats, towards the fact, face-on, plummeting in one of those late stonking twentieth century stadiums, a bedroom, although formal performance in this instance is, perm, a blur to watch.

The, co-operation, necessary to heat up, that which might have tuned both friends and a broadening community, teasing the vanishing shelf of 'the lot'.

To know, thrive.

Implicate creatures, an ear to wall with, it seems that the paying, is of over - enhanced attention to the bizarre.

Consider, lovely gully becoming humane, and once upon mouth landscapes preen surfaces of tongues within rocks, locating beyond the woods to cling which hunters weed, revealing undulating pathways of in quotation marks 'ancient forests' crying "technically prepared!".

The ice cream blubber sprinkled with sunstruck amber.

Today, well was it a moth in the shade or her hand's hand, touching herself in a night leeched from tidal detritus.

A mile, of.

```
bea  gull
 m   boo
```

Conversation and a quarter of one pound less than the necessary required to make a settlement into the heritage re-enactment of what was anal once @Saxon.gland.uk, adapted to re-appropriate remains, or that which is embodiment of flaw, eroding beyond the coastal road, the seas, as, an eyesore, foaming with luminous waste.

Of which, writing and then crossing ~~and~~ out replacing with retyping **and**, would 'act as' caustic scrim to scribing eyes and replenish the mashed stalks in our harbouring veins.

Even the frames of those adverts, between and within, the distortions grown close, thoughtful weaving assumptions of overlap, cruised our outlines, mapped their towns of terms, in and, by, erm . . . blink, re . . .erm blank - plenishing, feeding back a demotic dancer overlapping seam zipping them, cleaned their own component parts, and taxied to 'The Kebab of The Smokeless' and hand-drawn flare structures, pivotal facts, finely drowned their corridors of terms, in tribal broth, plastic behaviour.

Not dangle that would-be different, them harp wand "the brand of my liquid is old", fit sings the damned within implicit.

This page, another pale and tilted, to begun, have which, configured basement there, a.

From a barn, caught in the sloping eye, an old, story divorced and, wind block, roofing bouquet.

Electric smell which also scallops, sense, with shined hood fleecing trees, all summer, windblown the caramel electives of.

Embracing, dropping paper to the polished flooring leaves, glow theft blithe, sleepy punch and judy sunlit grey - blue glas berry town, sod stolid cold - door passages, drifting guck folded obnoxious emissions, taking advantage of daylit low cloud, the biomorphic cars moving, breathing thematic, the unnamed, blotted from blank, among rediscovered.

<<<<< Maps in hand, ringing that vigorous quilt, modelled inhabiting details with shadow, or inner vagrant colored, will wash for cash and catching the gleam into clubbed was.

pickled
whistle

A welcoming judge, the hum clubby.

Dispensing hey bub.

Smothered, would embed, what's recognisable, as a kind of slab, becoming futures of possibility, the, nuggets of suggestion, also passing, which can move than mark might steer.

Colour in, tattoo, the earth, a scar, in the surface of.

A sandbox, drawing, a hand, through, the child.

Too conveniently regarded as over-naturalised sewers from which these rivers, spring?

~~Cran omnte, nbe dubfl det, o, trv, n trs, f, tesle, s letd agt ht mvs oiotl, uhs, t qi, bitru oiain f, y dpie aito, h wt esaiy y ii, ht es o ofs a rod on hog, tak, na pth, n t si, fe or~~

```
                          si  le  nc  e
   ra  ve  r
                                          as    es
   se   nc   e        in          in  gl  as  h
     ex  ch  an  ge  s    wa  tc  h
   tr  il  l           pr  iv  at  e    se  ns  e
```

```
      im pr eg na bl e              if
 y     sh e
ry     ai   r
                   pr op ri at ed
                   ex hi bi t  sp oo  n
                   im  in in
      ga      p     er       bo
  nu      d                  co
 an     in                     ow
 so     am ho ss ib l          wo
      im po ss ib le   to   gr at if
y   sh e   cr av es
         pr    vi rt
         ap pr op ri at ed
            sa lu ta ti on


wa nt    in ks
so ld              gw la d    wo rl d
                      pe rf ec t
                       da te d
                    lo ng in g
```

```
     ji ng le   wa lk in g
 ev er yb od y
       ov er co
    ji
       ju
                     a
                     st
                     an
                     g
                     sk
                     ee
                      t
                      es
                        e
                          ac
                                    cr ap pe d
                                       ch il
th at   ju ng le              po ly
- p ol ic y
           ch an ge
         in g   a
```

po   sk
  pi   ee   ne
  ro   t   bo
  ke   es   of
          lu   fo r m
        to   ac ce pt   de
          r o pe d

we ig ht fo rm er ly se an ce in ri ve r
in du ct in g ro ug e in de nt at io n re
so rt in g as es se nc e in eu ro - en gl
is h ac co mo da ti on s ma de an ex ch
an ge wh ic h be gi ns am id ex - bl ok
en ru sh es to fr il l as h pr iv at e
se ns e of in an it y as vo id wa s qu
it e im po ss ib le to sa ti sf y sh e
wh o as wi tn es s to o an ge rs de ma
nd s

a ve ry vi rt uo us ch ao s
hi gh ly ap pr op ri at ed an d ob li qu e
ex hi bi ti on of va ri ou s ad jo in in g

re al it ie s   a   ga rd en er ' s   bo dy   of
        te nu re d   re gi on al   co nf li ct
an t   in ks   no t   un kn ow in gl y so ld   in
a   bo nd ed   wo rl d   at   la rg e   ri ng in g
a   pe rf ec ti on   wh ic h   in ti mi da te d
    ev er yb od y ' s   lo ng in g   to   ov er co
                me   un is on   un sa in

a   ji ng le   wa lk in g   ou t   of   th at   ju
ng le   a   co mm on   po ly - p ol ic y   sy st
em   of   ma rk et   pa rt s   ex ch an ge   ol d
re al is ms   qu ot in g   a   te le gr ap h   po
le   as   a   sk il fu ll y   ed it ed   pi ne   tr
ee   in   va ni ty   ne w   ro om s   ou t - da te
d   bo ok   li ke   an   im pr es si on   of   pr
is on   wh er e   va lu e   fo r   mo ne y   is
            el ec te d   to   ac ce pt   de

fe at s   la ng ua ge s   cr op pe d   to   se rv
    e   so ci et y ' s   ch il dr en   st op pe d

that, poppy gutted run off groove we re-configured, as
transmission

words one hoped, brain spun from waltzer, reeling
on the dangers of dancing the fog at the edge of this hay
making steam out of clay

and biting mouth

I'm f(am)(in)ished.

v i s i t e d
a b s e n c
e

it's all
too flaking
sad

the
uncut

where's the joy?

you mean i was
set up?

control's the flow

Other titles published by Reality Street Editions:

Nicole Brossard: *Typhon Dru*
Kelvin Corcoran: *Lyric Lyric*
Ken Edwards: *Futures*
Allen Fisher: *Dispossession and Cure*
Susan Gevirtz: *Taken Place*
Fanny Howe: *O'Clock*
Sarah Kirsch: *T*
Maggie O'Sullivan: *In the House of the Shaman*
Denise Riley: *Mop Mop Georgette*
Peter Riley: *Distant Points*
Lisa Robertson: *Debbie: an Epic*
Maurice Scully: *Steps*

Out of Everywhere: linguistically innovative poetry
by women in North America & the UK (ed. by Maggie O'Sullivan)

RSE 4Packs
No. 1: *Sleight of Foot*
(Miles Champion, Helen Kidd, Harriet Tarlo, Scott Thurston)
No. 2: *Vital Movement*
(Andy Brown, Jennifer Chalmers, Mike Higgins, Ira Lightman)

For more details, send an s.a.e. to the editorial address or e-mail
<kenedwards1@compuserve.com> or visit the RSE web site at
<http://www.demon.co.uk/eastfield/reality/>